sad shit about girls.

Brody
McVittie

this one's full of
one-pagers

that take a minute to
read
a second to feel
a week to get

a lot longer to
for___*˜

*get…

…get it?

…

A Tale of Two Parts:

Part One
the ways I swear I've changed

Part Two
Fuck you, I never could.

Part One

The ways I swear I've changed

I guess you could
think of this one

as something somewhat
resembling hope

like hope that I'm
not
completely and utterly
hopeless

and hope that I don't
fuck things up with
you

the way I terribly
tend to.

...

For the sake of
setting a scene,
let's suppose we're
at dinner.

Dinner, because I tend to take you there

when I'm trying to present as something other than

the completely and utterly hopeless

we've already established
I so clearly am.

So suppose we're in this establishment

and you look the way
you

so fucking
devastatingly
beautifully

 do

and let's suppose
I look somewhat decent
too,

all curled hair and
curled smile and

the kind of subtly
suggested danger

that hints at the kind
you're really in

because I'm really
not

(*kind)

but this part is about
how I've changed

and so the maybe make-
believe

is set to last
for the pages it takes

to imagine I'm
anything other than

the second part of
this book,

the part you can't
wait to tear into

the part that

--if you know me even
a little bit at all--

is more than most
likely
all about you.

...

*But first, dinner.

...

So there's this
girl, right?
And she's tall,
but not too tall
And she's got
great skin
And she's got
great lips
And her hair is
long and its
some kind of brown
or honey brown or
brown on brown
with belayage
blone highlights
and I

can't tell/don't care
because, to be perfectly honest with you
I can't get past her eyes.

You look at least as good
as the steak I order
trying to focus on
anything other than
tearing into you,

and so
this fucking fabulous
medium-rare meat
will have to do

until
the things I do
catch up to

the things I'm thinking,

the things I really want
to.

...

Her eyes suck.

Insomuch as they
don't suck at
all,
staring into mine
and from across
suddenly
uncomfortable
couches
and with a
ferocity

that only kinda
hides
under the sea of
whatever blue
went into
bewitching them.

And I blame her
momma
and I'll be sure
to thank/damn her
if I ever get the
chance

But, judging from
the way
she's burning me
from
the other side of
expensive leather
I probably won't

Because my luck
ran out
right around the
time she matched

Those pretty
fucking fabulous
eyes
on my suddenly,
woefully
insignificant
thanks-mom
bullshit browns.

wait

you mean
the violins playing in my
head

col legno
between your ears, too?

So she's winning

Genetic lotteries
and staring
contests

And even though
I really like to
fight

I'm throwing in
the towel
before the corner
rings the bell

because boxing
references are
just glancing
blows

between glances

to pretty girls
who give about as
much of a fuck

about silly self-
destructive
pastimes

as they do to
losing wars
I only just now
realize

we're in the
middle of waging.

Tired of telling sad
stories
and so I'm out at dinner
and out of the stories
I sometimes-always
typically tell

and

in lieu of fresh starts
I suppose you'll forgive
me
for being decidedly
silent

all

caught up in

sitting across tired and
somehow new tables and
trying to decide

if the 'I'll-be-better-
this-time'
is really this time

or

just the latest lie
I'm telling myself

before

the same sad story
I try to tell you.

Hope

is a funny thing

the way it fools you

into thinking this could be

anything other than

the trainwrecks that preceded it.

¥

And I do

(hope)

that you'll allow me the
unique and decidedly
understood
rare opportunity

to ruin your life

the way
the words
and the glances
and the
tiny little voice
in the back of your head

warn you

I'm

half my meal

and the subsequent drive
to my place

from really wrecking

more than the dress

you made the mistake of

barely wearing tonight.

...

I'm
tearing into this steak
(literally)

the way I'm tearing into
you
(figuratively)

figuring out
the ways I want to
(physically)

and so we're
(collectively)
two bites and two towns

away from the bed that
represents

the physical
manifestation

of the tearing down your
walls
the ruin-your-life

my malnourished mind

is dead set on
manifesting.

Want to be better
and so this book
is the last book

...because really
how 'sad shit about
girls'

can one guy really be?
...

I'm at dinner
and
off my meds
and
so I'm
so very sorry

for this
and
the mistakes
we're collectively
about to make

in lieu of
tasty meals
and
too much wine
and

the energy we share
sharing drinks
and
quiet desperation.

...

You've got those
**close down the restaurant
eyes**
and we did,
because they're sweeping
the floors
under and around us,
and you and I don't care
the way we don't care
about anything other than
exchanging those
what's behind the
glances ;

the kind that have me
wondering
if looking into those
close down the restaurant
eyes
is something I could see
myself doing

for days long after
this day,
the day of my first/last
date

since you made dates
about as necessary
as subtly sweeping floors
to suggest we get up and
leave.

You look like something
out of a movie

I watched back when
watching movies was
something

the cruelty of things
would relent enough to
let me.

So you and your
Disney Princess hair

and your

sometimes blue/sometimes
not

pretty little contact
lens/less
Disney Princess eyes

give me the kind of hope
I've been missing

since
VHS tapes in the eighties
preceded the
existentialism
that inevitably comes
both years and seconds

after tapes about Disney
Princesses

stop in the rewinding.

And I guess
that's the perfect
metaphor
for the running out of
time

you looking like
something out of a movie

is about and too.

...

Home Sense scents

and a lack of common

are about all we have in,

but we remain

fucking with each other
and over distances

only bridged digitally

on days when the songs we play

remind us to,

and with each other.

For the record, your sad
outweighs mine
and
you've got a few more
tattoos, too
so
I'll just sit here and
acquiesce

to your somewhat silent
superiority;

as if those eyes and
that ass

could fool any of the
everyone-else-at-the-
restaurant

that you're something
other than
more than I almost
deserve.
...

tacos and tequila and you.

we talk
easily and often
and

the digital distance

is masked by the
endorphins that come

when I come and get you.

And even though
you don't drive

and your town is too many
towns
away,

there's not a moment I
won't
head your way and for

the shots of tequila I
take
when I take mine.
...

little less intense than
that

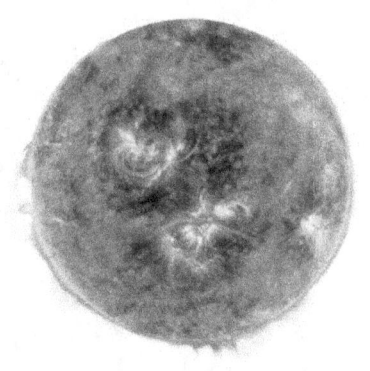

(but not much.)

You love
people where you're from
about as much as
the food we discuss their
superiority over

and so

I'm over here
sitting all not-exotic
and wondering

if my tasteless-by-
comparison
abject failings
could somehow fool you

into loving me, too.
...

simpin' ain' t easy.

Your accent
and
your ass
are tied

for
the things I love and
think about

most often
when I
(often)
think about you
and

I hope you don't
think less of me

and
for
manifestations and
manipulations

of words
other than
'I love you.'

...

She's got those
delete your DMs
eyes

is there anything
better
in the whole wide
world
than
tequila on thursday
and
girls with face
tattoos
?

please don't make this book about you.

sucker for
seafoam eyes
sideways smiles
&
not so subtle
sins.

Blame the storm
or
my overly-stimulated
synapses
or
my overly sensitive semi-
sane sensibilities
but you in
those glasses
and
that dress

have me imagining
the unholy and even less
healthy

array of emotion
releasing

unrepentant rage

the physical
manifestations

your unrelenting eye
fucking
just most assuredly

(and twice as literally)

fucking guaranteed.

...

dis/connect

I can't build houses
but I can twist a
tongue
hard enough
to trick you into
believing

I'm capable of the
anything more
than the next to
nothing

my two weary hands can
hold

knuckles bent and torn
and better suited

for the breaking
that kept these hands
both busy and with

the opposite of
construction
I spent all my time
deconstructing

So I'm sorry about
but
I can't offer you
anything more tonight

than rough hands
and cold whiskey

I can't build houses.

...

Hideously scarred

(just as scared).

I've ran fingers through
every color of hair
kissed all the kinds
of lips
there are to kiss
I've endured the
spiteful gazes
of the many mothers
who
saw right through the
gazes
that fooled their
daughters
into gazing back
months of years before

their gazes back
inevitably looked just
like
the looks on the faces
of their look-just-
like-them
mothers.
...

writer, muse.

Nobody tucks me in
and terrifies me
quite like you.

She's all
soda and storms
coke bottle body
hurricane eyes

so I'm sitting and
sipping
*simping
in weather better
suited for
thunderclouds and
overly-caffeinated
beverages

body buzz
side by side

  & seated

in the eye
of this particular

pretty downpour.

I'd pull my second favorite tooth to be with you.

I hate your eyes
for being that much
better than mine

and I guess the rest of
you is too,

but you fuck with me
in the way Jesus and your
parents and anyone who
has ever even remotely
interacted with me

tells you not to,

and so me and my
less-than eyes
and my

less-than reputation

thank you
and for the fucking
with

that's got you risking
the
over
Fucking Monkeypox
has me worried about
having to write a new
volume of
'Quarantine
Confessions'

the way

you're
worried about me
having to write a new
volume of
'Quarantine
Confessions'

because I maybe didn't
quite mention

how fucking mad
I am about the way
the rest of the world
and you

turned out the last time
some pandemic gave me the
freedom

to write about that very
same thing

you up and took from me.

...

Terrible Timmy O' Shea was the worst kind of fuckboi.

he'd slow play
the ways
he'd fuck with
the women who
made the mistake of
fucking with him,

Terrible Timmy
O' Shea,

letting them love him
and telling them he
loved them right back

loving them just
enough

to gaze lovingly
at the various other
women

foolish enough to look
his
terrible
terrible
way.

So for the rest of the
-however fucking many-
pages this book turns
out to be

when I say
someone's on some
Terrible Timmy O'Shea
shit,

please rest assured
said shit is plenty
terrible.

Trust the process
just a wee bit more
than
you try to trust me.

you've got
the most delicate little
Incredible Hulk™ hands
I've ever seen.

And, as contradictions
go,
it's easily the
most charming of your
many,

so Hulk Smash™ me
the way
you're

squaring up to,
here with me in the good
part

of the inevitably
good-to-bad
ratio your frequency
has me
frankly terrified into
feeling
each and every time

you tiny little Hulk™
hand hold me.

...

Call this
the first of many
forthcoming warnings
about the reality of
fucking with
Terrible Timmy
O'Shea.

Timmy O' Shea
loves all your stories
&
Timmy O' Shea
likes all of your
posts

Even the ones you post
in between the
onslaught of ass pics

you sometimes always
post;

yeah,

Timmy O'Shea engages
the stories about your
dog
and the posts about
whatever views
you lack the viewpoint
to effectively
understand
and more importantly
pontificate upon
the way you certainly
do,

--in between the ass
pics
Timmy O'Shea

(and almost everyone
else)
most certainly
prefers.

So beware,
Timmy O' Shea
and his terrible
levels of engagement

--best believe he's
after
what you spend hours
and investigations
about
complimentary lighting

highlighting

he's after that ass,
and most assuredly
nothing else.

So by now
you're getting the
sense
that 'the ways I
swear I've changed'
are quickly revealing
that I haven't really
changed at all.

I know
this one is like the
last one

but you were too,
and there's books
about her

so
here's one about you.

...

There's a formula to
this
The sad books about
girls
And the sins that
Cause the writing of
the next one.

So sorry
I was better at
English than math,

because breaking your
heart

and then writing books
about you leaving and
breaking mine

Is about the only
thing
I was ever really
really good at.
...

I can see the end
coming,

car crash on a snowy
street,

all "hold still, this
will only hurt for a
moment."

Part Two

Fuck you, I never could.

yeah, I'm the worst
but of all the boys
you've loved longer
and since

I'm the one you read
about
when the 'want you'
hits harder than

that time I showed up
at your place

on some 164bpm shit.*

*If you get it,
you really get it
and you know messaging me
is about three steps
south of
getting it
all over
again.
...

you like to leave me
voice notes
in between leavings

and you leave them
knowing I'll listen
over and over

to the ways
I failed as a man
and the ways you hope one
day I can change

and it's sweet
because we both know I
can't

but something in your
voice
has me writing notes just
like this,

trying to tell you
I wish I could see

what you sometimes still
see in me
south of the last time
you stopped the recording
that promised you'd
never leave me

another voice note

ever again

on the way to waiting

for the next time

you most assuredly do.

...

In the last seven months
I broke
my nose
—twice!
my rib
and my
seemingly-unbreakable
ability to weather
all of these assorted
breakings.

And it's not the boxing
you always told me to
stop
before I break something
that finally broke me

no, that designation

belongs to pretty little
you

and for breaking
the only thing I had
that kept me going

all those years before I

finally give/gave up
today,

some seven months

after you and

your terrible little Hulk
hands

went ahead and broke it.

...

So who's Terrible Timmy

now

and

really?*

*here's a hint, in case I'm annoyingly a little too vague

--it's you.

You're fucking Terrible Timmy.

Admit it
as far as
not-famous
absolute failures go,

there's no one
you'd rather read about.

...

Collected musings
for the absent
and absent minded

...

Here's to
broken balconies
cotton candy sunsets

and the boy
you broke on and under
some Sunday before

the inevitable Monday
bad break ups
broke you down to,

too
...

I find comfort
in the otherwise-engaged.

For the sake of both
pretending and some
semblance of clarity,

this is the part
where I unrelentingly
whine

about the ways you did me
wrong.

...

No,

my poetry is not the
problem.

Go on,
tell him you post the sad songs
because you just like the beats.

coward.

I loved you selfishly,
because selfishly is the
only way
silly boys like me
ever really love.

but I loved you
the way I love you
still

and
I'd like to take this
incredibly indulgent
opportunity

to thank you very much

for loving me the way
your
tiny little broken heart

let you
for the time you claimed
to
and the times to come
when you always
still
will.

...

Supposed to be

Stay Away

Somehow Mr. Everytime-
You're-Away-From-Him

Phone calls from cars
Driving directions you
swore you wouldn't

My way

Every chance you get and
because you
opposite of

Hate me

and I'm
opposite of

Stay Away.

Go on,
post another sad song
turn around and tell him
you just really like the
beat.

...

Not every song called
'haunt me'

Slaps

the way your tiny little
hand wants to

But the sentiment stays
something like the scent
of you
smothering admittedly
selfish sensibilities

Attacking me
amidst the clever
's' words
I fail to come up with

to leave the lingering

You and your semi-
sentimental
sweet little hauntings
play amongst the sad
songs
on the playlists that

promise

I'll never hear
that particular word
again

and

I'll never get
over you.

...

A broken heart is the
   easiest to feel

         &

The hardest to heal.

                ...

Absolutely yes but
 probably not.

 ...

Seldom Solace.
...

Big Billy Thunderhooves,
big on rabbit holes and
diving down

stirring up trouble and
tangentially-associated
tears

dragging up
the fuck forgetting
he knows his thundering
not so subtly encourages,

All

"bitch call me,
you know this one's
about you."

You rent room in the hole in my head,

All elephants and indignations

Reserving thoughts of how you
Take up almost every-all of them

You and your
Pretty little
Elephant-sized
Occupations

split skulls & soul
aches.

...

back turn no turn back.

...

insouciance is a motherfucker.

...

because
medium
and
maybe

were the worst words

you
ever
said.

...

because you know your new
book sucks.

...

Weaponized sadness.

...

My reputation
Precedes me
Unsettles you
Impedes us.

...

I took a picture of the
sunset
every day for a year
on some what-the-fuck-is-
wrong-with-me shit

Hoping that if you ever
came back
You'd have a
scrapbook/recap
Of all the nights it
turns out we didn't miss

Staring at sunsets
The way we used to and I
still do

Standing stubbornly and
alone and on balconies

So that one night I might
no longer have to.
...

You're weak and I'm
weak
and so
'Stay away from me'
is just some song
MGK sang on and about and
maybe didn't mean,
either.

After all, foxes make
meaning to be mean
harder than the resolve
in your voice
when you swear at me and
about how
you're over me and us
and

your position on it will
never weaken
until the weekend
when weakening
is two shots of rum
and taking another shot
at needing me
the way you
really need to.
...

You blame
accents and broken
English
but the actuality of it
is,

The words you use
to put me down

Kinda just makes you an
asshole
in every tongue you
twist.

...

Wild eyes
and
sometimes blue, sometimes brown
was just one of the tricks
you used in your tricking.

encapsulating
insecurities
in the tiny little layers
of plastic

you looked at me through

stirring schemes

behind off-colored eyes

clouding visibility and
likely judgement

in the making up of a
mind
that took advantage of
how I didn' t.

...

You asked me out
to be the fair
it turns out you
couldn't

because you said
the kinds of things
in courtship and
confidence

that succeeded in
really kinda hurting
mine.

So I'm blocking you
or about to

and when this comes out

you can read about

the ways you succeeded
in co-authoring
this latest volume of
misery

you amusedly created
with cutthroat eyes
and semi-sideway smiles.
...

Hang it over my head
kinda like
you used to
hang it over
the end of my bed.

...

You said I lied to you
at least one hundred
times

which is funny,
because we hung out
decidedly less than
that

And although you
and your nights away
were tied to the
questionably reported
truths

I believed in you

the way we both
recognized
I so desperately
needed to

back when
I only sort of
needed you.

...

Tried to catalogue
all the things to
dislike
about you,

from that hair between
your eyes

to the hair between
your thighs

and even though
I overlooked
the more glaring
of your

poisoned words
and
attempts to break me
down,

it's down to
the things you do
over the things you
didn't
that made me leave
when you wished I
wouldn't.

...

In case you haven't
figured it out

I'm still hurt about
it.

...

If this shit was an album
(instead of a collection of frankly whiny poetry):

Tracklist

1. You're about as authentic as the color of your contacts.
2. /mad shit about girls.
3. November pain.
4. That hair between your eyes (has been staring at me all night long.)
5. Haram is my middle name.
6. Fake tits & feelings.

...

We share
birthdays & broken noses
though the way we got to
both
may have been different
by decades & degrees.

So it's a shame shared
sentiments
& hidden feelings behind
them

couldn't keep this from
being
something behind us too,

trauma from broken things
reflected upon
when
that next day comes
around

& we simply don' t share
it.
...

Cover scars
in tattoos
and a less-permanent
sense of self;

and just like the books
and girls
that preceded
this one

I couldn't tell you
what any of it means.

...

Come on Billy
you're more than
twelve pages and the time
it takes

to write something that
can represent

the holes you put
yourself in
always trying to

put yourself in holes.

...

*Not whole.

Call this
 'assorted scribblings of
a semi-sane mind'

because this one
is the last one

before you

become the next one
that makes me pick up the
pen

in defense of
the feelings that

mistakes like this
inevitably make me

make again.

...

*If you're with me
by the time this comes
out

know that
the assorted whinings
and misrepresented
maladies

amount to
about as much as

the memories I can assure
you
I don't have

about the

sum total of the women
who made me

somewhat slowly
make **this**,

my latest and
arguably greatest

little literary mistake.
...

goddamned right it's about you.

...

Eight abs
(you're welcome)
and
sixteen volumes
and
one don't-look-at-me
lazy eye

and all it adds up to
is a decidedly drained

forty-something

failure

looking to absolve
significant sins

in and amongst your
hopes I could amount to

anything other than.

...

*If you've made it this far,

congratulations.

I know it's a lot but

--imagine how exhausting it feels

making me make it?

😉

Face tatts and fugue states.

...

You say
"you follow every whore
on Insta"
like it's a bad thing

what happened to
points for persistence
and
the sense of
accomplishment

that accompanies
being the one
worth settling down for?

...

Love songs

in lieu

of leavings.

you're stuck in my
head
like sad songs and
bone spurs

and though the hooks
that caused them

hurt more in the
punching than the
singing

you up and leaving
affected more than the
playlists

that hold down
the thoughts of you
beating me silly

hooks on hooks
leading to
books on books.
...

It's crazy
how bad I am at golf
math
and remembering why

I ever bothered
to fail at anything
other
than
failing to keep

all of my better-spent
and should have been
singular

focus

on staying in that bed
with you.

...

-hey I need you
(delete)
-hey I want you
(delete)
-hey don't go away.
(delete)

Like,
I love you

...but I don't even remember what you look like.

...

Once I get around to
getting this all
out of my head
and onto pages like
this

You're fucked
like you were fucked
before you got fucked

Some second right
after
the second

your sad eyes

tried to out sad mine.
...

Wasted all my best words

not convincing you to stay.

It worked

until it didn't

like Dad's old Chevy

...

miss

ms.

long drives

&

19 crimes.

She tells me she loves
me
on some
"I love you" shit

&

Proceeds to behave
With the kind of
Squirrel-headed
fuckery

That fucked our
chances
Of making anything

Out of the nothing
that followed

Mutually misspoken

"I love yous"

...

So words like
Prevaricated
Are worth the Google
You'll undoubtedly
have to

Some seconds before
you
Inevitably realize

You know exactly why
I looked them up to
Describe the ways

You tergiversated
the feelings

you maybe lie to
yourself
when you swear you've
shaken.

...

care taking since Take Care.

You haunt me like
October
and not just because
that's the month you
left me

And I miss the ways
I never had to miss
anything about you

By my side
And for three or four
Favorite months

Before spooky seasons

Extended for
the still-slipping

by days
since you said so.
...

man, sometimes I really miss you

burn the couches.

misguided gallery

insouciance

xvi

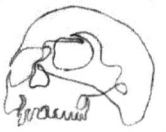

TRACKLIST

1. You're about as authentic as the color of your contacts.
2. /mad shit about girls.
3. November pain.
4. That hair between your eyes (has been staring at me all night long).
5. Haram is my middle name.
6. Fake tits and feelings.

lose the ones worth winning.

fractured mind, but you don't.

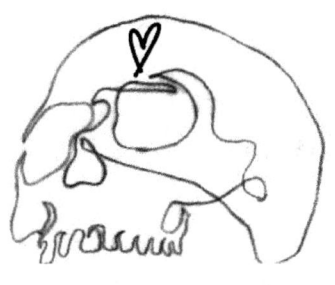

finish(ed).

www.ingramcontent.com/pod-product-compliance
Lightning Source LLC
Chambersburg PA
CBHW072052110526
44590CB00018B/3142